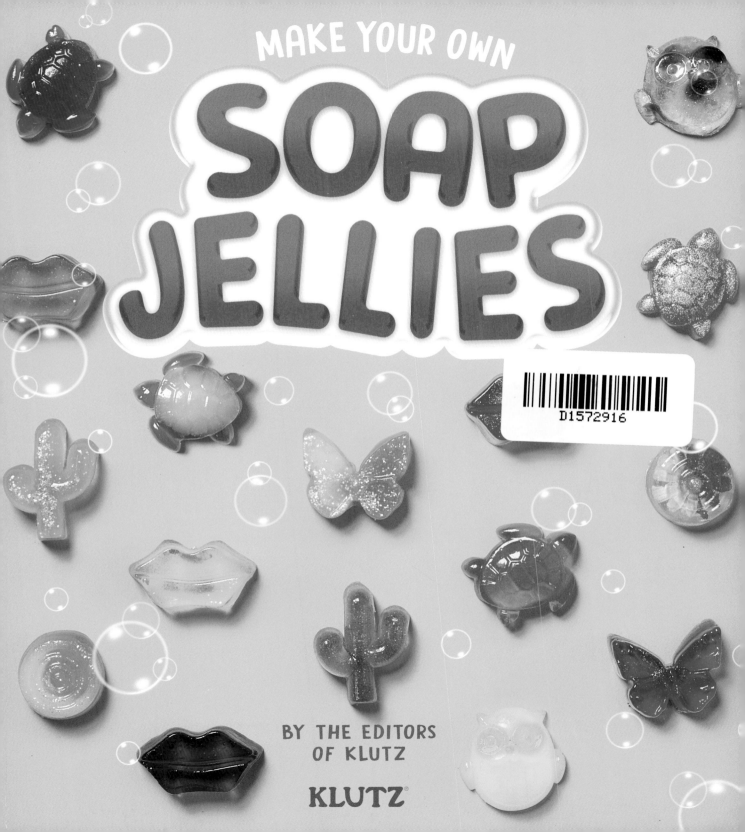

MAKE YOUR OWN
SOAP JELLIES

BY THE EDITORS
OF KLUTZ

KLUTZ®

KLUTZ®

KLUTZ® creates activity books and other great stuff for kids ages 3 to 103. We began our corporate life in 1977 in a garage we shared with a Chevrolet Impala. Although we've outgrown that first office, Klutz galactic headquarters is still staffed entirely by real human beings. For those of you who collect mission statements, here's ours:

CREATE WONDERFUL THINGS · BE GOOD · HAVE FUN

WRITE US
We would love to hear your comments regarding this or any of our books.

KLUTZ®
524 Broadway, 5th Floor
New York, NY 10012
thefolks@klutz.com

Distributed in Canada by
Scholastic Canada Ltd
604 King Street West
Toronto, Ontario
Canada M5V 1E1

Distributed in Australia by
Scholastic Australia Ltd
PO Box 579
Gosford, NSW
Australia 2250

Distributed in Hong Kong by
Scholastic Hong Kong Ltd
Suites 2001-2, Top Glory Tower
262 Gloucester Road
Causeway Bay, Hong Kong

ISBN 978-1-338-32150-0
4 1 5 8 5 7 0 8 8 8

FSC
www.fsc.org
MIX
Paper from
responsible sources
FSC™ C113204

We make Klutz books using resources that have been approved according to the FSC™ standard which is managed by the Forest Stewardship Council™. This means the paper in this book comes from well managed FSC™-certified forests and other controlled sources.

Bottle, fragrance, and scoubidou made in China. Foam booster made in Singapore. All other components made in Taiwan. 85

Ingredients/Ingrédients

Foam Booster/Mélange moussant: Water, Cocamidopropyl Betaine, Sodium chloride, Sodium sulfate
Jelly Powder/Gelée en poudre: Sugar, Glucose, Carrageenan, Locust Bean Gum, Potassium Chloride, Potassium Citrate, Sodium Citrate
Dye Tablets/Comprimé Colorant: Water/Eau, Sodium Cocoate, Glycerin, Sucrose, Propylene Glycol, Sodium Palmitate, Sodium Castorate, Isostearic Acid, May Contain/ Peut Contenir (+/-): Red 40 Lake(CI 16035), Yellow 5 Lake(CI 19140), Blue 1 Lake(CI 42090), Titanium Dioxide (CI 77891)
Fragrance/Parfum: Benzyl benzoate, Methyl dihydrojasmonate, Linalyl acetate, Citronelly acetate, Hexenyl acetate
Glitter/Brillants: Polyethylene Terephthalate, Polymethyl Methacrylate

Soap jellies do not contain any animal by-products, wheat, gluten, dairy, or soy.

Safety Information
CAUTION: IRRITANT
FOAM BOOSTER & FRAGRANCE MAY IRRITATE EYES & SKIN IN UNDILUTED STATE.
Use only as directed; follow all directions in the book.
If components are swallowed, seek medical advice immediately. In case of contact with the eyes, rinse well with water.
Discontinue use if irritation occurs. If irritation persists, consult a physician.

Sécurité renseignements
ATTENTION: IRRITANT
LE MÉLANGE MOUSSANT ET LE PARFUM PEUVENT IRRITER LES YEUX ET LA PEAU À L'ÉTAT NON DILUÉ.
Respecter les instructions d'emploi; Suivre toutes les directives du livre.
Si des composants sont avalés, consulter immédiatement un médecin. En cas de contact avec les yeux, bien rincer avec de l'eau.
Cesser d'utiliser ce produit en cas d'irritation cutanée. Consulter un médecin si l'irritation persiste.

CONTENTS

What You Get

START HERE

HEY, GROWN-UPS...10

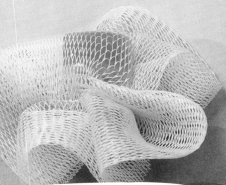

WHAT YOU GET

This kit includes everything you need to make 12 soap jellies in a rainbow of colors.

Jelly powder

Foam booster

Soap mold

Fragrance

MAKE YOUR OWN
SOAP JELLIES
FOAM BOOSTER
KLUTZ
568 Broadway 5th Floor
New York, NY

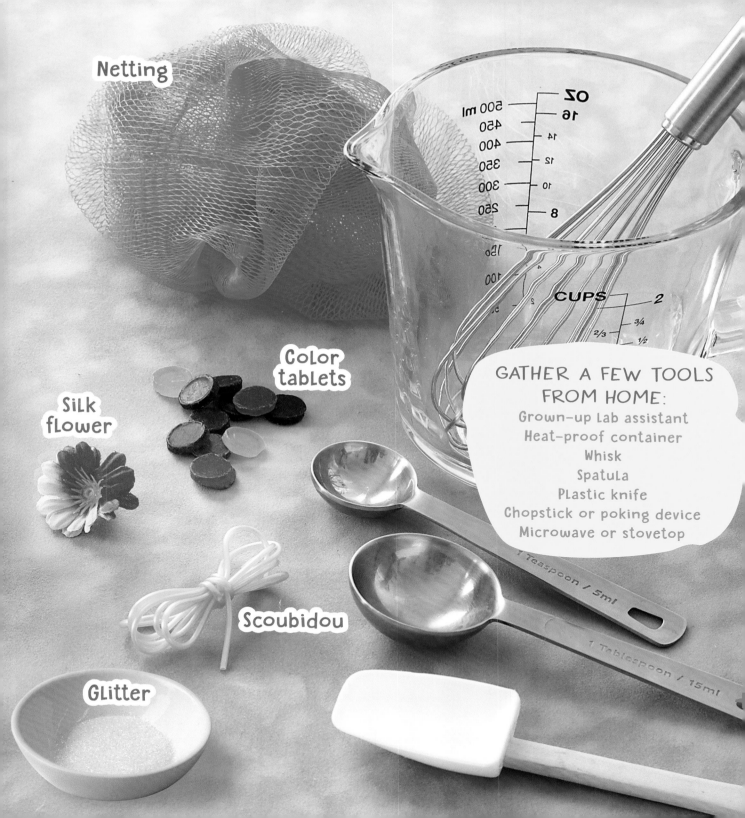

Netting

Color tablets

Silk flower

Scoubidou

Glitter

GATHER A FEW TOOLS
FROM HOME:
Grown-up lab assistant
Heat-proof container
Whisk
Spatula
Plastic knife
Chopstick or poking device
Microwave or stovetop

There are two ways to make your jellies: in the microwave (this page), or on a stovetop (page 9). Gather your ingredients and go to the method that works best for you.

BASIC SOAP JELLY

YOU WILL NEED

 5 teaspoons (25 mL) water

 Color tablet (in the color of your choice)

 Sweet pea flower fragrance

 ½ teaspoon (2.5 mL) foam booster

 1 teaspoon (5 mL) jelly powder

 Grown-up lab assistant

 Mold

MICROWAVE METHOD

Heat-proof glass container

Microwave

Small whisk

You'll need to work quickly. So have all your ingredients at the ready before you begin.

1 Measure and pour the water, foam booster, and color tablet into the glass container.

2 Microwave it for 20 seconds. The mixture will bubble up—that's OK!

Be careful taking out the container—it will be hot! Now's a good time for your grown-up lab assistant to pitch in.

3 Sprinkle the jelly powder into the liquid . . .

. . . and stir it all together.

KEEP GOING!

4 Add a drop or two of fragrance into the mixture.

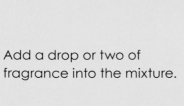

WORK QUICKLY!
It's best to heat, stir, and pour the mixture quickly. Sometimes the jelly will be more like a slushy if it sits in the glass container for too long.

5 Pour the mixture into the lip mold.

6 Now take a break! Let the soap jelly rest for one hour at room temperature.

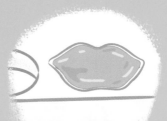

7 Hover the mold upside down over a plate. Use the tip of a plastic knife (or other flat tool) to gently flip out the soap jelly. It's ready to use!

While you're waiting, clean your container and whisk with warm water.

The mold shapes are all the same size, so you can use this recipe with any shape you'd like.

STOVETOP METHOD

Make sure your grown-up lab assistant is helming the stove for all your projects.

Small saucepan

Spatula

Small whisk

Grown-up lab assistant

1 Have your grown-up lab assistant heat the water in the saucepan over medium heat for about 30 seconds or until bubbles start to form.

2 Turn off the heat. Pour in the jelly powder and whisk it until the powder has totally dissolved.

3 Add the color chip and gently stir until it's melted into the liquid. Add a drop or two of fragrance and the foam booster. Stir them all together.

4 Turn off the heat, and pour the mixture into the mold. A spatula can help guide your mixture into the mold shape.

5 Clean all the equipment you used with warm water. Let the jelly rest for one hour at room temperature.

HEY, GROWN-UPS!

For your safety and well-being, please read the following information carefully. There are only a few important things to remember, so we made them extra-big and easy to read.

KIDS!

Get a responsible adult assistant for all of your soap-making. Make sure they read this page, and tell them there will be a quiz at the end.

Though soap-making isn't rocket science, it *is* a craft that uses hot liquids. We recommend that you, the adult, handle any materials that are being heated.

The projects in this book are made with powder that dissolves in hot water. You will need to heat water in every project. Hot water can burn if it touches your skin.

Never touch the heated jelly with your fingers. We recommend using a whisk or long stirring stick to stir your soap or to move any plastic toys you embed in the soap.

The plastic soap mold is not microwave-safe. Never heat or microwave the soap mold.

If you are sensitive to any ingredients in the fragrance, you can leave your soap unscented.

Let your soap-making tools soak in warm water to make clean-up easier.

Use only a microwave-safe glass measuring cup with a two-cup capacity.

WARNING!

If you accidentally spill the hot soap mixture on your skin, run the affected area under cold water immediately. In case of serious burns, seek medical attention!

USING SOAP JELLIES

You can use the jelly like a regular piece of soap to wash your hands. Or, break off a piece of the jelly and smoosh it into a bath pouf or washcloth to create a rich lather.

STORING YOUR SOAP

Soap jellies will last a few days if you leave them out on a regular soap dish. If you store them in an air-tight container, however, they can last for weeks! Always make sure to throw out your homemade bath products if they start to smell funny.

SO COOL

Soap jellies can be stored at room temperature. But if you want a refreshing treat on a hot summer day, try storing them in the fridge!

If you're storing these in the fridge, make sure to label them so other people in your house are not tempted to take a bite.

Make a Basic Soap Jelly first (page 6). It will help you understand all the tools that you need.

FLOWER RAINDROP

Feel fresh as a daisy! This clear soap is embedded with a pretty faux flower.

YOU WILL NEED

 5 teaspoons (25 mL) water

 Sweet pea flower fragrance

 Mold

Plastic knife

Chopstick

 1/2 teaspoon (2.5 mL) foam booster

 1 teaspoon (5 mL) jelly powder

 Faux flower

 Grown-up lab assistant

1 Use the water, jelly powder, foam booster, and fragrance to make a clear jelly mixture. Follow Steps 1–4 (pages 7–8).

2 Pour the clear jelly mixture into the round mold.

WHAT'S THE MATTER?

Scientists tell us that there are three states of matter: solid, liquid, and gas. So what the heck is wiggly, wobbly gel? It doesn't seem to fit into any of the three categories.

Gel is actually a web of solid molecules (like your jelly powder) suspended in liquid molecules (like the water and foam booster mixture).

The jelly powder molecules swell up when you add hot water, and they spread out into a matrix, or network. When they cool, the molecules hold the water in place.

WHAT'S IN YOUR JELLY POWDER?

The jelly powder is made from carrageenan (kair-uh-GHEE-nun), which is made from a type of seaweed that grows in the Atlantic Ocean. It puts the wiggle in your soap jellies.

SEAWEED IN YOUR ICE CREAM

Carrageenan is found in a lot of processed foods, like ice cream and almond milk. Food scientists (people who invent processed food) use carrageenan to help different ingredients thicken or stick together. You'll see carrageenan and similar gels (like xanthan gum) listed in the ingredients section on food packaging.

Be careful. It will be hot!

3 Carefully drop the faux flower into the mold, so you're looking at the back of the flower. Do not touch the jelly liquid!

. . . The flower will gently sink to the bottom of the mold. Use a chopstick to give it a nudge if it doesn't sink.

4 Let the jelly cool for one hour. Then flip the mold over and use the tip of a plastic knife to gently release the jelly. The flower will be embedded in a clear "raindrop!"

SOAPY SURPRISES

You can embed any waterproof object inside a soap jelly! Look for small toys, erasers, or other items without any sharp edges. Make the jellies clear, or add a color tablet to hide the surprise.

DISCO CACTUS

These sparkling soaps are squishy—not spiky! You can add glitter to any other soap jellies. too.

YOU WILL NEED

 5 teaspoons (25 mL) water

Green color tablet

 Sweet pea flower fragrance

 Grown-up lab assistant

Chopstick

 1/2 teaspoon (2.5 mL) foam booster

1 teaspoon (5 mL) jelly powder

 Pinch of glitter

 Mold

Plastic knife

1 Make a batch of green jelly mixture, following the steps for a Basic Soap Jelly (page 6).

(page 6)

SOAP SAFETY

Your grown-up lab assistant should be handling any and all hot equipment.

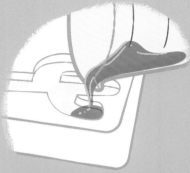

2 Pour the mixture into the cactus-shaped mold.

3 Wait for the cactus to cool slightly, about one minute. Then sprinkle a bit of glitter into the jelly and move it around with your chopstick or a toothpick.

4 After one hour, the jelly will be cool. Flip over the mold to let the jelly drop with the help of a plastic knife. Hold your arms like a cactus and do a little disco dance to celebrate!

HOW TO USE

The cactus arms will break off as you wash with the soap jelly. Each little piece is the perfect single serving of soap! And don't worry: the glitter will wash off.

DOUBLE POUR

Every soap looks unique with this technique!

 10 teaspoons (50 mL) water divided

 Pink color tablet

Orange color tablet

 Sweet pea flower fragrance

 Grown-up lab assistant

 Chopstick

 1 teaspoon (5 mL) foam booster

 2 teaspoons (10 mL) jelly powder, divided

 2 measuring cups

 Pinch of glitter

 Mold

 Plastic knife

1 Make two batches of jelly mixture in two different colors, following the steps for a Basic Soap Jelly (page 6).

SOAP SAFETY

Your grown-up lab assistant should be handling any and all hot equipment.

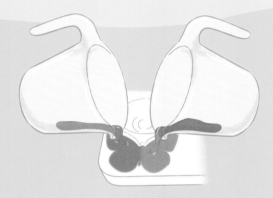

2 Hold one container in each hand and pour the jelly mixtures *at the same time.*

If it's hard to pour at the same time, ask someone else to hold the second cup.

3 STOP when the liquid reaches the top of the mold. If you like, add glitter now (page 17, Step 3.)

4 You have enough jelly mixture left to make a second double-poured soap jelly. Repeat Steps 2–3.

5 Wait one hour and flip out the jellies (using the tip of a plastic knife) after they have cooled completely.

You will have leftover liquid after making this project. You can use it to make another jelly.

TWO-TONE TURTLE

Layer different colors of jelly to make an adorable sea turtle.

YOU WILL NEED

 5 teaspoons (25 mL) water

 Teal color tablet

 Yellow color tablet

 Sweet pea flower fragrance

 Mold

 1/2 teaspoon (2.5 mL) foam booster

 1 teaspoon (5 mL) jelly powder

 Grown-up lab assistant

 Plastic knife

1 Make a jelly mixture, following the instructions for a Basic Soap Jelly (page 6).

(page 6)

2 Pour the jelly mixture into the turtle mold, but STOP when the shell is full. Pour the leftover mixture into another shape now, to make a second jelly.

3 Wait about two minutes until the shell has cooled a bit.

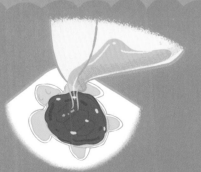

4 With a clean container, make another jelly mixture in a different color, and pour it into the turtle mold, all the way to the top.

5 Let the jelly cool for one hour, then flip over the mold and use the tip of a plastic knife to release this friendly turtle into the wild!

TIE-DYE OWL

Melt mystical-looking swirls into your soap jelly as it cools.

 5 teaspoons (25 mL) water

 1 teaspoon (5 mL) jelly powder

 Pinch of glitter

 Grown-up lab assistant

 Fork

 ½ teaspoon (2.5 mL) foam booster

 Sweet pea flower fragrance

 Blue color tablet

 Pink color tablet

 Mold

Plastic knife

1 Make a clear mixture, following the instructions for a Basic Soap Jelly (page 6.)

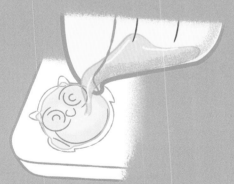

2 Pour the jelly mixture into the owl mold.

3 Place the soap chip flat on your work surface. Spear a fork into the chip.

4 Holding the fork, gently dip the soap chip into the clear jelly mixture in the mold.

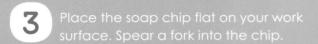

5 The heat of the clear jelly will melt the soap chip just a bit. Swirl the soap chip around until you like how it looks.

Some color combos—like orange and blue, or pink and green—may turn muddy if the swirls start to blend a lot.

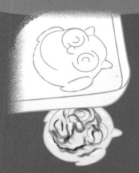

6 You can get fancy by repeating Steps 3–4 with another color. Swirl in a pinch of glitter, too, if you feel like it!

7 Let the jelly cool for one hour, then flip over the mold. Use the tip of a plastic knife to help release the jelly.

JELLYFISH LOOFAH

Add a little exfoliation (and extra cuteness) to your soap jelly by wrapping it in netting.

YOU WILL NEED

 Round soap jelly (finished)

 12" (30.5 cm) netting

 6" (15 cm) scoubidou

1 Place the soap jelly inside the netting, at the center.

2 Tightly twist one end of the netting.

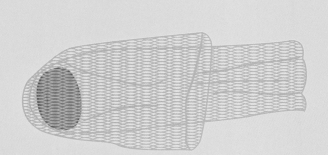

3 Pull the twisted side over the jelly, so it makes a little veil.

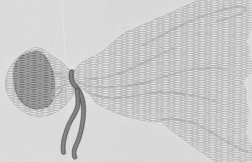

4 Wrap the scoubidou around the netting, just below the jelly. Knot it tightly a few times.

CUPCAKE POUF

Scrub your worries away with a sweet-looking bath pouf.

YOU WILL NEED

 Round soap jelly (finished)

Plastic knife

 12" (30.5 cm) netting

 6" (15 cm) scoubidou

 Cupcake wrapper (optional)

1 Cut the soap jelly into four pieces. You will only use one piece.

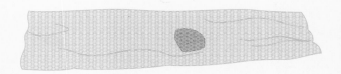

2 Place the soap jelly in the center of the netting.

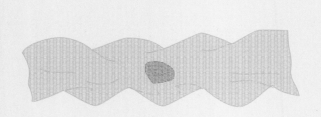

3 Fold each end of the netting back and forth, like a zigzag, until you reach the center.

4 Hold the netting in place with one hand. If it's tricky, ask a friend for help.

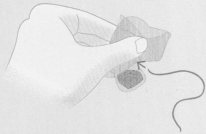

5 Push the scoubidou through the center of the netting, just above the jelly. This will take a bit of time. Then tie the ends in a tight knot a few times.

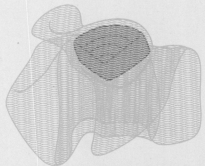

6 Pull on the edges of the netting until you like the way it looks. Put it in a cupcake wrapper, if you'd like.

BEYOND THE BOOK

There are lots of other kitchen and craft supplies you can use in your soap jelly–making adventures. Here are some ideas to get you started.

Look for ice cube trays with fun shapes to make different kinds of soap jellies.

Googly eyes turn simple circles into cute li'l frogs.

This citrus-inspired project is easier than it looks. Cut up pieces of soap jelly, place them in a large round mold, and pour clear jelly mixture to fill it up.

Sugar sprinkles can be added to your jelly mixture, just like you would add glitter.

Pour any leftover scraps into a round ice cube mold to make this intergalactic soap jelly.

HOMEMADE SOAP JELLIES

If you're making more soap jellies at home, you can use these ingredients to substitute the ones in this kit:

- Replace the foam booster with ½ teaspoon (2.5 mL) of liquid soap, such as your favorite body wash.

- Replace the jelly powder with ¼ teaspoon (1.2 mL) of carrageenan powder, which you can find in specialty food stores.

CREDITS

Editor: **Caitlin Harpin**

Designers: **Kristin Carder and Vanessa Han**

Technical Illustrator: **Kat Uno**

Package Designer: **Owen Keating**

Buyer: **Mimi Oey**

Photographer: **Alexandra Grablewski**

Product Development Manager: **Gina Kim**

Product Integrity Specialist: **Sam Walker**

Special Thanks to: **Stacy Lellos, Netta Rabin,
Hannah Rogge, and Kim Rogers**

Get creative with more from KLUTZ®

Looking for more goof-proof activities, sneak peeks, and giveaways? Find us online!

 KlutzCertified   KlutzCertified   KlutzCertified   KlutzCertified   Klutz

Klutz.com • thefolks@klutz.com • 1-800-737-4123